[1]

Annular

Dedication

This book is dedicated to my parents (James and Eunice),
maternal grands (Ross and Bertha),
paternal grands (Wade and Ella),
and the late Dr. A.M Sharpe.
Also, to those who
persevere in their artistry.

Acknowledgements

I would like to thank my wife, Krystal, for being
very supportive, patient and understanding.
Also, a ton of thanks to Robin Bryant, Gerald Jackson
and Selvy Cobb for their undying
critique and insight.

To Dr. Butler Brewton, who inspired me to write poetry
and my many coworkers who read my poems
and gave encouragement.

Poems

I.

II.

III.

IV.

Annular

I will go out into the night of day
And witness as your body gets in the way

In the way of rays of sunlight-
In the way of the circadian clock of crickets-
In the way of chaos and confusion
In the way of thoughts of men-

Then those who dare, in this brief swath of a miracle,
will slowly and carefully lift their heads in
totality and behold your majestic crown and rejoice in
the grandeur of the moment

Trees Felled (17 Parkland Fla. and Many More)

Some trees will never see the splendor and fruition of their
purpose
Many are felled before soaring and reaching majestic heights
never to give shade nor solace
Many an eagle or jay will never get the chance to alight upon
their lofty crowns and look down upon the ground
With roots having yet to spread, they will never branch to
their
truest potential, with sap running rich and wild
Saplings truncated, while yet dawn

A Native Son

This land is my land. For
I have trod barefoot upon
the red clay and waded in
streams where snakes abide.

And I've picked cotton,
peaches, blackberries and
hauled hay, from the red soil
from which they sprang.

Climbed steep, wet hills with
brother, sister and my brood
of friends and slid down in
rapid descent.

Walking a hilly and meandering
pothole infested road, I would
see the chain gang taming sprawling
growth and repairing years of decay.

And I would descend and walk
toward the house from the bus,
only to hear the name Coon yelled,
as it rolled off.

The Young Man in the Cemetery
(Darius)

He was looking intently at
Three graves in the cemetery.
Looking as though he would
Find something. There was
A sense of expectancy about
His gaze.

He was only twelve-years-old,
Handsome, chapped-lips, a member
Of the choir and gradually approaching
Puberty.

One of the graves made a
Monument of red clay dirt
To his deceased uncle,
Who died just recently, as a result of
Getting choked while eating.

The other two graves housed his
Mother and brother, victims about
A year ago in a bloodletting crime
Of passion.

This young man related to me
In a matter-of -fact manner,
About what happened to each,
As though detached from all
Familial ties.

Too young to ingest the full import
Of this tragedy, and how it will
Impact his young life, he remains
Stoic and undeterred.

Yet he sings and sways on the
Choir to *Hold to God's unchanging*
Hand, with a rhythm that flies in the
Face of reality and defies all
Odds.

Young Darius, the embodiment
Of the innocence of youth, and
Resilience of spirit; coming
Up, on the rough side of the mountain.

Surnames of Strength
(A Tribute to Black History Month)

The agricultural wit of Carver,
The oratorical skill of King,
The fiery persona of Malcolm,
Do bid a people sing.

While the strong leadership of Douglass,
Noteworthy scholarship of Dubois,
And ample patience of Washington,
Have brought us thus this far.

The brave, heroic feats of Tubman,
And noble courageousness of Truth,
The *sit-down stand* of the lowly Parks,
Gave birth to hope and proof.

Wise counsel dispensed via Marshall,
With gritty soulfulness growled by Brown,
A lofty anthem led by Basie,
Throughout the land resounds.

Marching

They marched. Oh, how they marched.
Some two hundred and fifty thousand strong,
Going to lay down their burdens by a
Reflective pool under the watchful gaze
Of Lincoln.

Coming from north, south, east and west
To call a nation out and set it straight.
By bus, train, plane, car, or foot, they came.
En masse they stood, with heart in hand that
We may now stand.

The march that made the world stand still
And listen to a man with a dream. "Tell
'em 'bout your dream, Martin," shouted
Mahalia, and he did.

With unprecedented eloquence the prophet
Uttered words that echo beyond lines, districts,
Boundaries, seas and stars. Yes, he had the vision
And courage to lay it down! Told how it's supposed to be.
Told how woefully short we measure up to
Ideals laid down by men who also had a dream.

They marched so strong and with an unwavering
Purpose that doors once unhinged swung open.
Doors which give us unimpeded entrance
To further the march. Marching with an awareness
That Martin, Medgar, Malcolm, Emmit and a cloud
Of countless saints and martyrs, ushered us in.

The Back Porch Well

On the enclosed back porch was the
Well, from which water was drawn.
Teeth-chilling cold water
When placed to one's lips.

Water, which was felt
Meandering its way
Down the throat and innards
To somewhere deep below.

Water, which came from a well
Bored deep into the earth
To extract the elixir of life
Which Mother Nature gives.

Chilly, cold water, which calmed
our thirst on hot summer days
From too much work or play
In the cotton field.

Into this back porch well we would
Yell and listen to our voices
As they dissipated into the
Bowels of the earth.

This well into which we would
Drop a pebble and watch
The ripple smile and expand from an
Ever-widening circle within a circle.

The back porch well,
That held the bucket and dipper,
From which we would partake
Of the sustainer of life.

From Without and Within
(9/11)

They came tumbling down,
The twin towers of New York.
Symbols of man's ingenuity
And America's grandeur.
Crumbling to the ground as
If being imploded from within, but
We know it came from without.

It came without loved ones
Saying, "I love you," before
Leaving for work or school, not
Knowing this would be their last
Earthly embrace.

It came without anyone being
Prepared for such a dastardly
And diabolical scheme; without awareness
That some would have to make a
Ghastly decision between being devoured
In a towering inferno or plunging
Some one hundred or more stories to their demise.

It came without brave hearts
Being timid but making the
Ultimate sacrifice for others
And for the greater good.

But from within is where
We must begin the towering

Work of rebuilding ourselves
And our nation. Within is where
We must begin to rebuild from without.

God in the Storm

God speaks in a variety of ways;
one way is through a storm.
I heard Him say, *I'll show man his*
trifling ways are not mine and not
what I created him for.

I heard Him as He blew through Houston,
Texas, ravaging and destroying whatever
was in His path. Destroying black, white,
old, young, rich and poor. Certainly not a
respecter of person.

I also heard Him say, *you look on the outward*
appearance, but I look upon the heart.

Many times the obvious gets lost in the fog.
We all have the same color and texture of those
things within: blood, spit, mucous even shit.
But we close the door to our hearts when we
look through the window of our eyes and see only the
façade.

Division creeps in and destroys our intended image;
erecting walls, barriers, restrictions and fences.

And I also heard him say, *I will show them.*

Altar Call

Spring is here much too soon, much too late
As the dandelion and crocus awake
And wren, jay and bluebird sing a familiar refrain

It's time to be redundant:
Plant, cut grass, play in the Sun
Plant, cut grass, play in the Sun

As Lady Gaia genuflects towards the Sun
We too must pay homage to this celestial rite
Something put into motion eons ago by the unmoved mover
Let us move to the altar of the Burning Eye

II.

Ambition
Where there is no vision, the people perish.

It's that intangible one must possess to make a mark along
the way. It cuts a swath through the thickets of time,
providing
passage for many. Propelled by a force unseen, yet real,
misunderstood, yet indispensable.

It's what launched man to the moon and gave Edison his
incandescent vision. It helped to erect Richard Wright's
prose and Frank Wright's architecture. Helped to
orchestrate Ellington's greatest compositions.

It helped to spawn movements and crusades and rested
firmly in the heart of Denmark Vesey. Sojourns in a man's
soul who now sits in the most powerful seat in
the world.

Inspires the picturesque vistas from the eyes behind
the lens. It's the apple that opened the gates of
communication globally and moved Renoir to paint the
rolling rapids.

It's how we live and have our truest being and something
you must have from the get-go or find along the way.

A New Harvest (In the Wake of Mother Emanuel)

Let's bring out the old mule
to turn a dying land over,
and prepare the field anew
for a new harvest to cover.

Let's till a row of kindness
fertilized with abundant hope,
and stamp out weeds of rancor
where bigotry tends to cope.

Let's bring out the aged plow
to cultivate and lay bare,
the evilness and hate
that many spread and share.

Let's reap the harvest sown
in the early days of spring,
and tell the laborers now
they can lift their voices and sing.

We are not Afraid

-Affirmation-

To go into darkness alone and walk
the untrampled path,
afraid we are not.

Nor to face situations which cause one
to shudder and doubt their own sense of agency,
we stand not afraid.

Ready to face the clarion call of the trump as it
blares that note of judgment,
still not afraid.

No, we are not afraid and can never be.
For to be shackled by fear is to be on a desolate
plantation, stripped of manhood and disenfranchised of
hope.

Tomorrow, Too Late

Tomorrow might be too late.
Too late to see the reluctant bloom
of the Camilla; too late to notice the latent
moment of a miracle; too late to
to hear the cascades of the Reedy River;
too late to mend broken fences, promises
and dreams; too late to tell those near, how
much you love, care, and esteem; too late to
hear the ocean rush to the shore; too late to feel
the warmth of the hearth; too late to bring together
what's apart; too late to hold the peacefulness of
surrender; too late to value what's truly tender.

Resurrection

Time to start anew and bring
Back things once dreamed
And visualized to fruition. Time to
Plant seeds of hope as the faded
Grass gives way to new life. This
Is a day and moment of completely new
Beginnings; fresh and pregnant with imminent
Possibilities and transcendent desires. This is when
We must roll away the stones from our catacombs
And raise our prostrate spirits onward. To resurrect
What was lost and dormant to reality; and like the man
From Galilee, walk on water and calm the sea.

Dum Spiro Spero (While I breathe, I hope)

While I breathe, I hope that on this day
we can hew out of the mountain of indifference
a stone of conviction.

While I breathe, I hope that the gates of
hell not prevail in a society unraveling
at its seams.

While I breathe, I hope not to see our
verdant and majestic land transformed
into a jungle of sprawl and concrete.

While I breathe, I hope that the attitudes
of prejudice and bigotry that still exist be
replaced with a paradigm of openness
and tolerance.

And while I breathe, I hope that some day
soon, the remnants of the Orangeburg Massacre
will be given an official, on-the-record apology
from the seat of our government.

Dum spiro spero.
*The motto of South Carolina

Extension

You stand in the backyard with rake in hand,
with a distinguished hairline. I hear about your
athleticism and basketball prowess, yet I see a missing
link which one must bind.

Your grandfather is the one, but I too must stand
in and serve as a coupling to that missing link.
My tomorrow and yours are intertwined in an intricate
web of destiny.

Your father would have wanted this: someone to serve
as an extension to his missing power.

Kneeling

The tree that fell didn't really fall,
it was genuflecting towards the gravidity of the moment.

III.

Bring Them Out

Those devilish dudes of misbehavior,
bring them out.

Like slavery and Jim Crow, you've gone
through the gauntlet of oppression.

All must speak now to unveil the assholes
of indecency.

Tell about the stronghold of harassment and
the partakers of exploitation, the pain of a glass ceiling.

Bring to light what was done in darkness.
The moment is right, like a helping wind-

like a propitious stream-
Bring darkness to the marvelous light.

No More Gray

You have shown your ass.
Like you're the brazen giant of
Greek fame. You walk around
with unbridled hubris.

Should have seen it coming, mama
told me about your kind but ears can
be like a tunnel, in one, out the other.
Your colossal ego is frightening.

Like you're the eighth wonder of the
world. ISIS could use someone like you,
Someone maniacal, delusional, damn crazy.
Dreadfully damned.

No more shades of gray, you're in high-
deaf now, crystal clear, 1080p. Your train
is about to derail, from a track that crosses
a bottomless chasm.

Rain men

It's raining as I write, provoking memories
Of yesteryear and what rain does.
As the rain would hit the earth, puddles
would form, creating in my young, imaginative
mind, rain men.

Mama Donald and I would sit
on the back porch and watch them
as they crossed the street or made their
way to work. Some even carried umbrellas.

Why carry an umbrella when you're already wet?
These weren't your run of the mill rain men. They
had legs, feet, arms and heads.   Falling from heaven,
walking on earth.

Saw two even making love against a silhouetted
leaf. Some would splash and dissipate into other
rain men, precipitating their own unique communities,
obverse to ours.

Rain men don't care what others think;
they just walk against the rain.

Sleep   *(To sleep, perchance to dream)*

Heard you sleeping with a pleasant rasp
Don't know but maybe in the key of C
Divining a note allowing passage
You talked with your father

Yes, he was there
Imposing figure in bold relief,
 Inhabiting your dream
As you pirouetted, frolicked and capered about

Enamored by his presence, son, daughter,
With their cherubic faces laughed aloud at your
Headlong glee. Suddenly disconnected from
The umbilical cord of your dream

You turned and sighed quickly
Then slowly morphed,
Leaving this realm,
Catching up with your father down the road.

Sorry Won't Do

Words spoken and muddled from
Unclean lips and a cloudy vision
Not partaking in clarity of thought
And how words sting and wound

Sorry won't do

Not being able to un-ring the bell
Once rung tolling with a peal of
Regret, befuddlement and a strange
Kind of wonder

Sorry won't do

The door left open when told to keep
shut things undone which beckon
Our attention a shoelace untied which
Could make one fall

Sorry won't do

Yet we must with strength forgive ourselves
And seek the forgiveness of those we trespass
Against and look within the chamber of chambers
For a clearer and better way

Because sorry won't do

Insidious

They pop an offshoot of the poppy-
Lortab, OxyContin, Vicodin, Horse-soothing an ache, easing a
pain. While at the same time being lured by the siren which
enchants. Up and down, back and forth. Enthralled by the
manacles of addiction and dependency.

When up, euphoria and ecstasy.
When down, despair and despondency.

Many take the expressway arriving quickly to their
destination
as the opioid travels the Jetstream of their veins. Flying
some
Forty- thousand feet high in their mental skies, they begin to
descend and find themselves among the clouds.

Unable to find their bearings, disorientation sets in as they
slip from the contrails of their flight and find themselves
upside down, headed towards a mountain, too late to right
the plane and pull back on the wheel and ascend.

Stolen Years

King heroin was fine as long as it didn't cross the line.
As long as it stayed on my side of the tracks it was cool.
Get locked up for years messing around with this
forbidden fruit. Many have succumbed to its seductive
allure and are now housed in a cage while sons and
daughters are bereft of fathers. While wives have
 to play the role of dual parent and work three jobs
just to make ends meet.

But now things have changed since it's now on your side of
the tracks. The king has been downgraded, lost some of
its statutory power. The king is now considered an epidemic.
Deemed so because it has reached "mainstream" population.
With a wave of some magical wand the power that holds sway
has its way, again. Wonder if that wand could be waved to give
back the time and years to those locked behind closed doors?

Years that didn't see little ones graduate from grade to grade;
years that didn't see Johnny catch that winning touchdown or
hear Robin's recital; years that wives wept on their husband's
birthdays; years that were stolen.

Beltless

I saw him with boxers showing,
Trousers sagging, climbing a slope,
Unaware, not even knowing,
Quite a buffoon, a sad, sad joke.

Cellphone in one hand the other
Hoisting his britches nigh waist high,
What's happening to our brothers,
Why comport yourselves so awry.

The Strap

It lay on a chair,
brown, black and thick,
a reminder of days,
when we had to take our licks.

An attitude adjustor
and correcting rod,
this leather material,
Brought us closer to God.

Not spanked but whipped,
by a fiery father,
in his hands,
held the future, to all others.

Whenever I see
this whipping tool,
I now realized,
it changed a fool.

Spring

You come in with a bouquet of brilliance,
showering our senses with a kaleidoscope of images:

> the flag as it waves aback a turquoise sky-
> a hovering bumble bee, waiting to bore through
> wood-
> the iridescent waters of the rolling river-
> the repetitive call of the Northern bob white-
> a velvety touch of the garden rose-
> the pungent smell of a fresh-mowed lawn-
> the succulent taste of a vine-ripe tomato-
> the gentle caress of an early morning breeze-

> Such sexy images spring rains down on us.

Turning Point

Autumn brings in a montage of splendor
with its turning leaves of yellow, red, orange
and brown.

The big oak and maple exhale from summer's
singeing rays, while the vinca, blue salvia, encore
azalea, black-eyed susan and autumn joy display
their radiance.

It's time for bales of hay, pumpkins, the spider's
snare everywhere and Halloween.

We're in a spinning top turning its back on
our source of strength.

It's a season to fall for.

Bewitching Hour

Some will come for trick or treat soon, dressed in
Other selves, bringing their own baggage of desires.

Parents will escort their little goblins to our front
Door where treats will be given, or will they?

Maybe someone will come dressed as a little Donald Trump
Where I will summarily lead him to the backyard and
Place his head in the guillotine. . .

Or maybe a little O.J. will show up wearing little gloves
That don't fit. In that case, I must acquit. . .

Or maybe I will stay this enchanted evening and watch the
moon, The Belt of Orion, a new day coming soon.

Forlorn

It's gray and dreary this cloudless day
Where leaf and cone now fall away
Where tall green grass has lost its smile
While big man oak shed leaf awhile

Where once our love blossomed with hope
Now dry and withered cannot cope
Where once lo those joyful years
Comes now this autumn fraught with tears

Christmas Without (A Sonnet for Christmas)

What would Christmas be like without a tree
Or the splendor of lights on top our roofs
Or the sight of a child on Santa's knee
The scene of Rudolph and his friends on hoofs

A taste of eggnog seasoning one's tongue
A yuletide card that wishes and brings cheer
The melody of a carol now sung
Oh, the quaff, of a freshly crafted beer

What would Christmas be without joy or hope
The colors red, white and green everywhere
Probably like someone strung out on dope
Or living life like you no longer care

Christmas means more than just O Tannenbaum
It's a time of new life for everyone

Glad You Were Born

These are the words that resonated:
glad you were born. Birthdays come
and go, with many trying to squeeze
events, dinners and special memories into
this, their day of arrival.

Uneventful would describe my two score
and ten plus five; having to work and teach
a class, receiving cards and calls throughout
the day from family close and those who extend.
But glad you were born is something that stuck.

Not to diminish the significance of cards and calls,
but words spoken with sincerity and forethought
make one pause. Pause to give thanks to this someone
who validated my meager existence and gave
credence to my sense of agency.

Glad you were born is all I needed to hear. In a
rapidly changing society of values, mores, technology
and ideology, it's good to find solace in the right
phrase, delivered at the right time. Keep the cards,
skip the dinner, never mind a party, just let me
know that you're glad that I was born.

A Thief in the Den

Love weddings, the foundation, promissory note,
love ones in search of the Golden Fleece.

Ministers, priests and pastors, delivering rites,
and catechisms.

But when you take advantage of humility,
we must engage.

Saw, felt you trying to pilfer my wife's exposed Ben
Franklin. And she, expecting grace would lead her home.

Instead, you, a charlatan, imposter, a downright thief, tries
to strip my Athena of her moolah.

Can't believe one could have been so bodacious and
brazen to play cards underneath the Sycamore tree.

But you tried. We'll continue to pray for your kind:
a thief among saints.

A Fading Glory

It's not the same school I went to
nor the same band I heard play years ago.

Not the same fanbase nor the
same uncurbed enthusiasm.

Our glory is fading, our brand
no longer dominating.

We have succumbed to being
relegated to the dustbin of history.

We need an institutional paradigmatic shift
of what a university should be.

Maybe a new State of Mind is what's
called for in these days of thine.

Modern Development

I see the backhoe, cranes and other earth-moving equipment of Caterpillar; equipment of destruction and reconstruction.

The old pine, oak and maple tree, shed their tears this autumn, as they're being uprooted and dispossessed of their habitat.

The buck and doe must now find new fields to forage and roam; the wren, swallow and cardinal, new treetops to alight.

A trench is carved deeper into the earth where pipes will be laid to transport human waste and bring water into this once pristine land.

Children will skate on pavement and play basketball where the fox used to trot and the opossum used to strut.

And these newcomers will help to clog the already congested highways and roads, creating a thrombosis of traffic, seeking a valve for relief.

All of this sacrilegious displacement, in the name of development.

Joel on the Wheel (Walks on Wassaw)

Those tidal marshes, sandpipers, bald-eagle-nest,
Blue Nose dolphins and the wake of the boat

Joel, my captain, enthralled us with his
Cultural wit

We rode on a highway of salt and
An undulating terrain of mist

A Cul-de-sac of bliss

Better for it all

Change

Change rolls in on the
wheels of inevitability,
crushing under its weight
those refusing to accommodate its arrival.

It blows in on the
jet stream of Mother Nature,
creating havoc and chaos for those
ill-prepared for its ferocity.

But it also provides much needed
sustenance and growth for those
in need of sunshine and rain, producing
the bountifulness that Mother Nature gives.

Change is the catalyst for
growth, the enzyme of the
universe, promoting
continuity and maturation.

Change is necessity, blowing
north, south, east and west,
from the prairies of America
to the shores of Mozambique.

IV.

Angel on East Fair Isle

There's an angel on East Fair Isle,
who watches and cares about us all.
With her gentle words and gestures
of a love profound, only God to her,
do and did, his love abound.

There's an angel on East Fair Isle,
whom I've spoken with and shared a
smile, touched her corrugated veins,
watched her blush, upon East Fair Isle.

There's an angel on East Fair Isle,
with Charlestonian ways and a pleasant
smile, with a heart of gold and mind so wise,
this angel Betty, love personified.

Aunt Rose

We laid down Aunt Rose just the other day
in a halo of pink: pink suit - pink hat - pink casket.
Being interred in the soggy soils of Winter Park, Fla
It was a righteous Homegoing

Know she was proud as her grandson eulogized
her work, a work of planting, cultivating and harvesting-
Buttressed by his mother and sister this young man-
dressed in military splendor- was a testimony to her
sowing and reaping

And her soon-to -be 80-year-old brother-in-law, Uncle J.R.
stirred the congregation with an old standard: Amazing
Grace, as he controlled and elevated the spiritual
temperature of the Mount

We traveled as a family to pay homage to a genteel
soul, Aunt Rose, as witness to laying her down in
this peninsular land of Florida,
and seeing her rise in her offspring

Ella

One shoe she wore
had a slit in its side,
this woman knew
goodness as her guide.

This shoe-cut-hole
opened up for a corn,
but like a rose
this was her thorn.

Goddess like looks
skin soft and light bronze,
meek and modest
ever since being born.

A culinary queen
as many have heard,
mind sharp and keen
and lovely as a bird.

My Sunday teacher
grandmother, too,
I still reach her
in dreams of life anew.

Kudos to Our Fathers (A Fathers' Day Tribute)

This is our day, for the men
who accepted the challenge.
For the unsung heroes who do
the messy and sometimes unrequited
work of creating structure and
sustaining an institution.

For the blue collar, who toils in the
oppressiveness of heat and the frigidity
of cold. And for the white collar,
who riffles through reams of policy and
red tape.

This is for those who didn't leave,
but stayed for better or worse; who
looked their man child in their tiny eyes
and saw the stars; glimmering with hope
and promising a brighter tomorrow.

Yes, this is our day, we who carry the seed
of posterity. We who make the difference
in a more perfect union. We who set the tone
and pitch of an award winning song.
Let us fathers, still fight on.

For Those Who Gave

For those who gave their last full measure of devotion
we stay forever in your debt. A sacrifice too courageous
and valiant to reimburse, too numerous to count, too
memorable to forget.

Yet we stand on this bright threshold of a new day searching
for ways that mirror and commemorate those truncated dreams
of the fallen who walked unafraid into the lion's den. Your
anthem has yet to be sung.

For the unwitting, who thought surely, they would see family
next furlough; for the forgotten, who took the brunt of blows as
the Edmund Pettus Bridge was crossed, and for the remembered,
whose spirit lingers and inhabits our steps.

These are they, the Centrifugal Force of Courage, an Axis of
Adoration.

Hands

I've seen your hands as they cared
for your father and now your mother.
Hands that have generosity written
in each palm.

There is an abundance of kindness
in your hands, hands which wave, point
hoist, and pray. Hands not made by man,
but by the Maker.

I've seen your hands as they've picked
tomatoes, or wiped dust off of a neglected
table. Ever so mindful to the task at hand,
present, in the fading moment.

Your hands hold our past and present
at the same time, showing us from whence
we've come and where we stand. Hands of a
heroine, saving lives and inspiring souls.

Hands that clap in church,
that care for a patient, that snap
green beans and cook collard greens.
Helping hands, that heal our land.

(written for Jackie on her birthday)

Mountain Top

Remember the days we would hide in the canes, pick cotton
or help Daddy Ross toss wood on the back of the old Dodge truck?
These are days that still hold sway. Didn't need town or
city because we had Cobb Road. Yes, a lost paradise where plums,
muscadines, grapes grow on vines divine.

Where the old mule, Red, would sometimes escape from his
stable only to be lured back in by the old patriarch.
Where Mama Bert would sit, scribbling like a scribe; playing her
role in a movement called civil rights by helping to swell black
voter turnout.
Eating turnip greens and cornbread with the tips of her fingers,
we were unaware of her noble status.

Then you led Bertha's Choraliers, striking chords on the piano and
raising your bombastic baritone, resonating throughout the
church.

> *"Dear Woodmont High we love you so.*
> *We'll think of you wherever we go".*

These are the beginning words to our shared alma mater.

Then, you took off and went down I-26 to the small town of
Denmark and found a new alma mater in Voorhees College.
You would come to the bigger town of Orangeburg, occasionally,
to pay me a visit.

Then one day you strutted down the aisle and got your papers: O
HAPPY DAY!

You came back home to serve, serving with a committed heart and spirit. But from a distance Ohio beaconed and you answered. Leaving behind family, friends, places and faces; you continued your work in a strange land.

So "Top", we celebrate you and this your day of arrival. And I'm glad to have such a Big-Black Wonderful cousin.

Happy Birthday Day, Mountain Top!

(Written for Michael on the occasion of his 60th birthday)

Steve and Tiny (Waters of Love)

To have and behold for 40 years is truly a blessing.
And just as the Saluda and Broad Rivers pour into
the Congaree, so have you, Steve and Tiny, poured
your undying love and presence into the streams of
all our lives.

Forty years of wedlock bring its challenges; for it's not
in times of bliss that define a marriage, but in times of
the abyss.

For I have seen you in those Hartsville Days, Bonnie Forest
Days, Irmo Days, facing your set of challenges: relocations,
strife, loss of mothers, brother, sister, and son. But
somehow,
through an unremitting grace, you forged on.

So, it is on days like this, we pause, honor and give thanks,
to this, your union.

Thankful for being family and friend; thankful for the
meteoric rise of your daughter, Shauna, whom we are all so
proud of; thankful for how you always receive us into your
home with warmth and affection; thankful for how you
always keep your bar well-stocked; thankful most of all for
being authentic and true, wonderful and new.

May the waters of your love continue to flood our streams
and riverbanks.
(Written for Steve and Tiny's 40th wedding anniversary)

That Girl

Introduced to you by your best friend who has now long since left this light and resides amongst the stars. Such an auspicious evening was that day; I wearing purple and you sitting on a throne (Nefertiti and Athena would have envied your beauty) in a place that used to *dazzle* many.

I coy and you aloof; yes, we were friends before lovers, and that has made a difference. Different poles, New York and South Carolina, rural and metropolitan, being brought together by a force stronger than magnetism.

You come from good stock, so I shouldn't be surprised by your station in life. For you are the wife that men launch ships for and fight wars over. Your sons and daughter may not yet know the gift and blessing that they now behold, but they will one day.

Your star hasn't set but continues to rise; rising to a majestic height. For you have made your mark in both the private and public domain. And I've seen you gravitate among notoriety and the common. Seen you sweep floors and wipe down chandeliers. Seen you laugh and seen you cry. But I'm so glad to have found *That Girl*.

So, this is the day that the Lord has made; let us now robustly rejoice and be glad in it!

(Written for Krystal on the occasion of her 53rd birthday)

A King in the Queen City

It seems like I knew you before we met. A knowing
without really knowing, a chance encounter. Serendipity.
Fate. The gods must have preordained that our worlds
would collide.

With our 10-speeds we would strike out over hill and
stream, stopping maybe for a 12-pack of Black Label
or ride through the park during *the golden time of
day.*

Challenging each other in a game of chess, I would
listen as you would relate to me your latest
exploits, living vicariously through your every
word; a player and gentleman.

Yes, and I've seen you on days when you've felt
as though you were destined to the lot of *Sisyphus*:
having to push a boulder up a hill, only to have it
roll back again.

But over the hill did the boulder finally go. That's
when we began to take wings and slip these surly
shores and *raise Tuskegee.*

My friend, you are all that came plodding through
the rain before you. Your parents, grandparents, great-
grands, great-greats, didn't pick cotton, dam rivers, or
lay rail in vain.

They knew that royalty was streaming through their veins

and one day a king would crawl his way out of the fungal
abyss and plant himself into the now.

And I have learned from you, Gerald, several good
moves in the game of life. I rejoice in having
met you and the infectious joy you bring.

Regality personified, my friend, regality personified.
That's what you are. A king, who holds court, in the
Queen City.
Friendship is Essential to the Soul

(Written for Gerald on the occasion of his 57th birthday)

Crucible

We stand on a precipice
                              -or near it
A cacophony of pleading, railing, hoping

A strident rainbow coalition
A spectrum of promise waiting on fulfillment

Not yet one among many but a penny,
Divided among nickels, dimes, quarters
And oh yes, the almighty dollar

We are a choir singing off key
Devoid of harmony; a writer searching for his voice;
A proposal waiting on an answer

Standing on this precipice we look down into
A crucible where an array of metals mix, meld and
Mold into an unknowable known

An experiment framed in hope and a justifiable
Belief in forging one's destiny is in this pot, boiling and
Spilling over onto the burner

Thank You

for buying and reading my poetry collection *Annular*.

Please post a review at the store where you purchased it.

*

To find out about future publications, speaking
engagements, book signings, please follow me at:

DwightDonald@gmail.com
Twitter: @DwightDonald1
https://www.goodreads.com/user/show/79983551-dwight-
donald

Please know that this author respects subscribers and
does not inundate them with sales emails.

Biography

Annular is Dwight Donald's first collection of poems. He comes full circle as he shares insight on his childhood, significant others, historical moments, inspiration, seasons and musings.

His works have appeared in *USA Today*, *The State*, *The Charleston Post and Courier*, *The Greenville News*, *The Virginia Pilot* and *The Community Informer*.

Born in the county of Greenville, South Carolina, he attended the public school system where he graduated from Wood-mont High School in 1976. He furthered his education at South Carolina State University, receiving his B.A. in 1980.

He is married to Krystal Donald and they have three children.

[69]

Made in the USA
Columbia, SC
31 August 2018